I0159214

BRAND YOU!

MASTER YOUR

SOCIAL MEDIA

A Step-by-Step Guide To Create A
Powerful Social Media Presence
To Establish Your Personal Brand

BY DIANE HUTH, MA, MBA

Book Cover Design by
K.Venkata RamaRao

Copyright © 2017 Diane Huth
All Rights Reserved.

No part of this book may be reproduced or utilized in any form or by any means,
electronic or mechanical, including photocopying, recording or by any
information storage or retrieval system without permission in writing.

Inquiries should be addressed to:
Diane Huth
Diane@BrandYouGuide.com
(888) HIREME2

www.BrandYouGuide.com

PUBLISHER'S NOTE:

This publication is designed to provide accurate information at the time of publication. It is sold with the understanding that the author
and publisher are not engaged in rendering legal, accounting or other professional services. If you require legal advice or expert
assistance, you should seek the services of a competent professional.

Any brand names or logos are used in an editorial fashion, and the author and publisher claim no relationship with or ownership of
other companies other than specifically noted herein. Any recommendations for action, vendors or service providers are the sole
opinion of the author. Names and contact information for résumés, cover letters, elevator pitches, broadcast letters, scripts or other
document examples may be based on real people, but their names and contact information have been changed to protect their privacy.

Published by

ISLA
Publishing Group

San Antonio, TX USA

TABLE OF CONTENTS

BRAND YOU!
TO LAND YOUR
DREAM JOB

Land your Dream Job with our **MINI BOOKS!**

7 Negotiate the Best Possible Offer

6 Master the Interview

5 Find, Apply For, and Get the Job Interview

4 Become a Master Networker

3 Find and Monetize Internships

2 Build a Powerful Resume and Job Hunting Tools

1 Master Your Online Presence

INTRODUCTION

YOUR SECRET WEAPON TO LANDING YOUR DREAM JOB

Finding and landing your ideal job doesn't happen by chance. You have to know the secrets of how to market yourself to land your dream job. You can learn and employ this unique set of skills to ensure you find a good job, get hired, and jumpstart your career. This book will teach you these skills, and share with you an insider's view of what it takes to be the one person out of hundreds of applicants to receive a coveted offer.

This is the first of 7 topic-specific eBooks which will guide you step-by-step through your job search journey:

MASTER YOUR SOCIAL MEDIA

In this step-by-step guide, you will discover many valuable insights including how to:

- Understand That YOU Are a Brand
- Discover What is Your Personal Brand Today
- Use Google – It's How You Track Your Personal Brand Development
- Master LinkedIn – Your Number One Job Hunting Resource
- Create and Distribute Press Releases to Drive Google Ranking
- Master Online Media – The 6 Key Social Media Sites Every Job Seeker Needs to Have
- Create Your Own Website for Powerful Personal Branding
- Manage Your Passwords and Login Information
- Harness Powerful Email Tools for Your Job Search
- Monitor Your Credit Report

…and many more!

Your dream job is out there somewhere. When you read this book series, you will gain the tools and insight to find where it is hidden, get your persuasive credentials into the right hands throughout the hiring process, help you successfully complete the various interviews, and negotiate a great employment package.

The learning here will help you greatly speed up the job-hunting process, furnish you with the tools you will need to succeed, and help you avoid the mistakes and pitfalls that hamper the job search of most people.

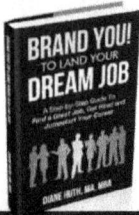

Get your **FREE** 15-Page Checklist

☑ *Specific, Measurable Objectives*
☑ *Increase Your Employer Response Rate*
☑ *Learn the Steps to Job Hunting Success*

www.HireMeNowPlease.com

And as a special gift for choosing this book, I am pleased to offer you a FREE Step-by-Step Career Guide and Checklist which is available for immediate download NOW so you can follow along chapter-by-chapter to track your progress. Go to www.HireMeNowPlease.com for your FREE DOWNLOAD.

1.
It's a Tough Job Market

The unemployment rate of recent college graduates is double that of the total population, and more than 21% of recent college graduates are either unemployed (7.2%) or underemployed (14.5%.) In 2014, 46% of college graduates worked in jobs that didn't require a college degree. And today, 15% of taxi drivers have a college degree. *Fortune.com* states that 48% of all Uber drivers have at least a college degree.

Money Magazine estimates that it generally takes 3 to 9 months for the average college graduate to get a job. And according to *Newsweek*, millennials make up about 40% of the unemployed.

But don't despair. Of the almost 3 million new graduates to enter the workforce this year, more than 2.2 million of them will find employment. This book will help you to become one of the well-employed professionals, working in a field you love for a good salary.

2.
What Compelled Me to Write This Book

I've worked in brand marketing for what seems like forever – more than 30 years! My career spanned 20 years in top-level marketing slots at a wide range of household-name companies including Johnson & Johnson, Frito-Lay/Sabritas, Carnation/Nestlé, CBS Cable and Mission Foods. I also sold multimedia advertising for 5 years, and held leadership roles with 8 start-up companies.

I am currently Chief Marketing Officer of Biovideo, pioneering maternity photography and videography services, and a Senior Innovation Consultant for Prodigy Works, a national consulting firm.

And in my spare time, I teach Marketing Management, Branding and International Marketing at 2 different universities in Texas.

While teaching marketing students during their final semester of college, I was stunned to find out how poorly prepared they were to search for and land a job.

They didn't understand the dynamics of a job interview, nor how to ferret out the unlisted jobs that go to people in the know without ever being posted on a job board. And none of them knew how to find and meet the people who would hire them. They simply didn't have a clue.

Because I had taught marketing classes at very different universities, I realized lack of preparation wasn't unique to one particular school; it was the same across the board. My students were bright, personable and motivated. But they didn't know how to write a persuasive résumé, prepare a memorable business card, police their social media pages, create a LinkedIn page, or find a mentor. Nor did they know how to network at professional events; and most had never attended professional trade associations where their future employers congregate. They didn't know how to give an elevator pitch, write a cover letter, or ace an interview. And few were prepared to dress for a successful business meeting or interview.

I learned that the Career Services team at each school offered students résumé reviews and help, career seminars, coaching, on-campus job fairs and more — all free to students. But for some reason, few students took advantage of these opportunities. So here they were, just months from graduation, with no concrete plan to get hired into that dream job.

My job was to teach them all about marketing, right? So I developed this program to teach them how to use all the marketing and branding skills they were learning in class to market their most important product — themselves!

First, I taught students in my classes. Then word spread, and I was asked to give the class — which had evolved into a two-hour seminar and then a four-hour workshop — to different classes and student groups on campus. Everywhere, the response was the same: students were amazed to learn precisely what they needed to do to stand out from the crowd and be selected for that one coveted job that so many people were applying for.

I received many requests for the presentation, and realized that just static slides weren't enough. So I decided to write down in detail the many tips and secrets involved in launching and advancing your career, so these valuable skills can be learned by anyone anywhere and at any age.

3.
How to Use This Book

The complete book – **BRAND YOU! To Land our Dream Job** – is a step-by-step guide which walks you in detail through the job search journey, starting with pre-search social media management all the way to successfully negotiating and accepting your dream job offer. This is a process which may take several months to complete. And each step depends upon successfully completing the prior step which lays the foundation for success in all subsequent phases of your journey.

I have edited the content to break up the book into 7 different micro-books, with each eBook focusing on one specific stage of your job hunt. And I have added lots of added content and much more detail on key steps than would fit in the full book.

You can follow the series step-by-step from Book 1 through Book 7 as you progress through your search, or you can jump to the specific micro-book that will unlock the secrets of your current job search stage.

However, I strongly recommend that you start from the beginning with Book 1 to make sure you are fully equipped with all the tools and insights needed to find and land your dream job fast!

<u>Find Lots of Resources and Links at the End of the Book</u>

At the end of the book, I have summarized all the resources available that I cite throughout the book, along with dozens of links to websites, resources, news articles, government stats, and much more. There's also a complete index to all topics in this book. So don't worry about visiting all the pages while you are reading; they all will be handy in the Resource section at the end.

Remember to follow along and check off your job preparedness status in your downloadable step-by-step Career Guide and Checklist. Download it now at www.HireMeNowPlease.com.

Get your **FREE** 15-Page Checklist

BRAND YOU!
TO LAND YOUR
DREAM JOB

☑ *Specific, Measurable Objectives*
☑ *Increase Your Employer Response Rate*
☑ *Learn the Steps to Job Hunting Success*

www.HireMeNowPlease.com

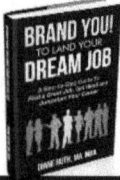

4.
Learn Job Success Secrets for Everyone

This book originally was written for college students getting ready to enter the professional marketplace. But it's not just for students and recent graduates. The insights, tips and recommendations are crucial for any professional in any field, whether just starting out, wanting to change jobs, or being forced to shift gears after an unexpected layoff or life change.

This isn't a static book, something to read and put away. Instead, it's an active guide full of step-by-step assignments to complete, and specific tasks you need to tackle now to get ready to find and land your dream job.

The book is available for college Career Services staff everywhere to help prepare their students to get hired. In addition to the book, you will find valuable information, free templates, useful checklists, and step-by-step tools at no charge at my website www.BrandYouGuide.com.

5.
Understand That You Are a Brand

You may not realize it but you are a brand. Everything that applies to branding and marketing a product or service applies to marketing yourself. The same principles that I teach in marketing classes apply to branding yourself to land your dream job.

You must create a strong brand name, a persuasive story, and a memorable visual presence; you have to communicate how you will add value, and define and exploit your competitive advantages.

According to Jeff Bezos, the legendary founder of Amazon, "Your personal brand is what people say about you when you leave the room." Your brand is your personal and professional reputation.

"Your personal brand is what people say about you when you leave the room."

--Jeff Bezos – founder of Amazon

It's very important that you take care of your reputation, that you nurture it and that you position it so that what people think and say about you is what you WANT them to think and say.

When you brand yourself properly, the competition becomes irrelevant.

In this book, you will learn how to position and sell yourself so you shine in comparison to the competition and make hiring managers say, "We want THAT person."

6.
What is Your Personal Brand Today?
An Exercise in Self-Assessment in Just 4 Easy Steps

The first thing you need to do is conduct a self-assessment to benchmark where you are on your personal branding journey. You will be working on building your brand awareness and image throughout the coming months as part of a successful job search. So it's important to see where you are now, to be able to map the steps to get you to where you want to go.

Follow these 4 simple steps:

1. Ask everyone you know how they would describe you in just 1 word – and why they chose that word. Make a game of it and post it on your Facebook, LinkedIn and other social media pages.

2. Copy each word into an Excel spreadsheet and sort by the number of mentions or in alphabetic order.

3. In the second column, write down the number of times each word is mentioned. Sort by the highest number of mentions to lowest number of mentions.

4. Then in the third column, indicate whether a potential employer or recruiter would consider that description or trait to be Negative (N) or Positive (P).

This is your personal brand. This is how others see you. It's a great place to start to figure out how to find and land that great job.

7.
Master Your Online Media Presence

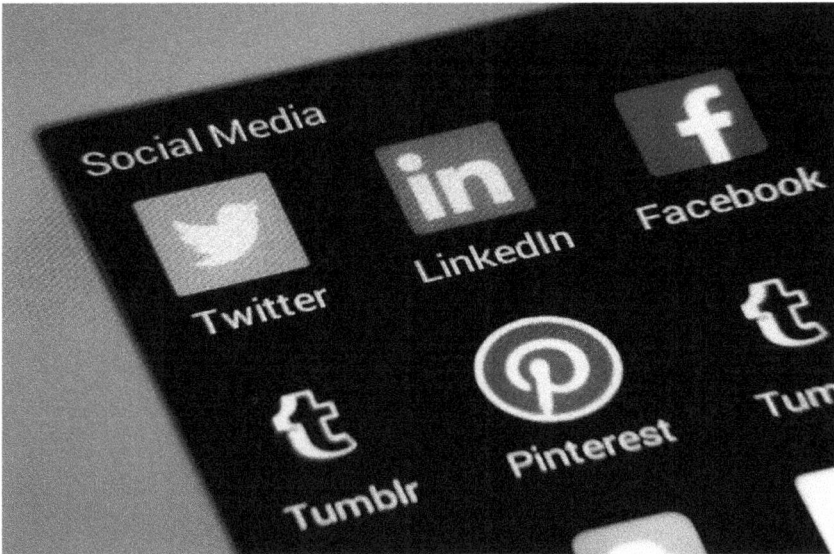

The first step in your job search is to master your social media presence. Think about all the different sites where information about you may appear to a potential employer.

One of the first things any employer or recruiter will do is to look at your social media presence when evaluating you as a potential employee. According to *CareerBuilder*, 51% of companies google candidates as part of the hiring and selection process. A recent survey by Microsoft found that a whopping 79% of employers now conduct an online search of candidates, and 70% of employers have rejected applicants for what they found online. This is in addition to standard background and reference checks!

So what is your personal brand today?

8.
Google — It's How You Track Your Personal Brand

80% of success
is showing up
... on Google.

Woody Allen once said "80% of success is showing up."

Today, 80% of success is showing up — on Google!

Stop right now and google your name. That's what any employer is going to do. What does your Google profile show?

- Can you even find yourself?

- Are you on the first page, or on subsequent pages?

- Are there many people with the same name? Or are you unique and listed at the top?

- How many times do you appear, and what is the content of the listings?

- Is there a good photo you want potential employers to see?

- Is there anything negative that you don't want an employer to find?

Go Google Yourself

If you don't have multiple favorable listings ranked right at the top of the search page, with great photos, you have work to do. We will work on establishing your professional name to fix this in Chapter 25.

9.
Use Press Releases to Stand Out on Google Search

Of course you want to show up prominently on Google, and be listed and profiled in a positive manner on Google (and other search engines.) Surprisingly, it's not as hard as you think. Google and all search engines have "spiders" that comb through millions of webpages each month, searching out any published information or stories, and then posting the links, whether you want them to or not. You can't control IF they will post about you — but you can influence WHAT they will post.

If anyone writes a story that's published anywhere and your name is in it, whether it's positive or negative, that story and your name will show up on Google practically forever. So you should proactively strive to secure favorable press coverage that will eventually show up in search engines so these are found first in any search.

One of the best ways to get ranked high in a Google search is to either issue a press release or be mentioned in a release or story. When you issue a press release, you prominently list your name, your phone number, your email address, and sometimes a quote — and all of that will get captured and listed on Google and other search engines.

I served on the Board of the American Marketing Association (AMA) for a number of years and I issued dozens of press releases — that still appear in my Google profile more than 10 years later.

So you should frequently issue a press release for just about anything — your professional association, a club, a social activity, even a church garage sale or a "news article" that you create on your own. This is the easiest way I know to get a favorable first page ranking on Google.

10.
Write a Persuasive and Engaging Press Release

A press release is a one-page document that clearly lays out newsworthy information in a format that makes it easy for a media outlet to create a story to share with their audience. Releases are always written in third person - *"readers will find"* rather than *"you will find."* A well-written release can be picked up word-for-word and inserted in a publication without editing. That should be your goal: to create such a compelling story that a local paper will print it exactly as you submit it. And of course you must have completely accurate grammar and spelling without any typos.

Writing a press release is a skill you can easily learn. There are 8 key sections to a press release - make sure you include them all in this order:

1. **Header:** Include the organization's logo, if appropriate, and optionally PRESS RELEASE in bold caps. On the far right, list contact information, flush right – name, email and phone

2. **Dateline:** Start with the date the release is to be distributed – indicate if it is "For Immediate Release" or for distribution on a different date.

3. **Headline:** Write the headline you want to see on the article in a target publication. Write a headline that is interesting enough to tweet. Keep it short and sweet. It is often printed in bold caps. Optimize your head line with keywords. Spend time creating a powerful persuasive headline as it will make or break your release.

4. **Location:** The city and state where the release is created.

5. **Sub-Head:** Provide more information to complete the headline. It should "hook" the reader into reading the next section. When read in conjunction with the headline, it should convey the full message of the release. This further narrows down the target audience; the reader finds out if this press release is relevant to him.

6. **Lead Paragraph:** Set the hook in the reader's attention with an interesting lead sentence. Keep the reader moving toward the objectives – key messaging and calls to action.

7. **Call to Action:** Once the reader is hooked, the call to action (CTA) instructs him what to do. It should be phrased in imperative language such as: call now, find out more, donate here, buy your tickets now, or visit a store today, for example. The CTA is designed to provoke an immediate response. The CTA link must be after the first or second paragraph. Also, refrain from posting irrelevant links on the press release so that the reader is directed to click the call to action link.

8. **Body Copy:** Provide all the information needed to respond to the call to action - provide the 5 W's – who, what, when, why, and where. Tell the story, add dimension and readability, with quotes, bullet points and paragraph heads in bold text. Give the reader reasons to keep going. Bold font and provocative section heads draw readers' eyes in, and build more attention. Provide a quote from a key person, executive or spokesperson.

9. **Boilerplate and Media Contact Information:** Establish the brand's credentials and give journalists the about-the-company details they need for the story. Include the web site, blog, and repeat the media contact information. A release is general ended by providing 3 hashmarks centered at the bottom of the release - # # # - to indicate the information is complete.

**Effective Press Releases:
The BRAND YOU! Advantage**

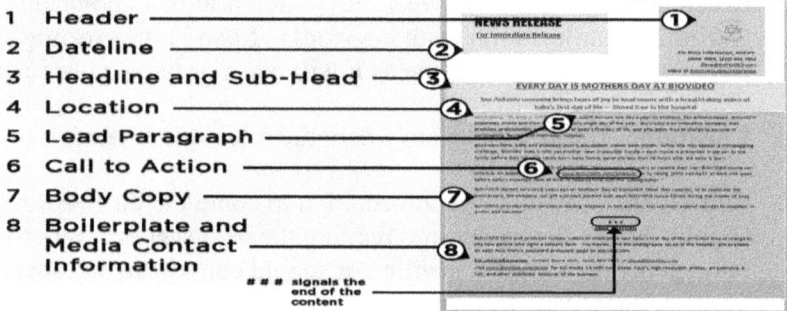

1 Header
2 Dateline
3 Headline and Sub-Head
4 Location
5 Lead Paragraph
6 Call to Action
7 Body Copy
8 Boilerplate and Media Contact Information

signals the end of the content

© 2017 Brand You! Guide

If you want help writing your release, contact us at
www.BrandYouGuide.com

Make sure you invest the time and energy to create powerful "hooks" to GRAB your audience so they continue to read sentenced after sentence. It's a funnel where you use a strong headline to capture initial attention, then provide more and more specific information as the release continues.

What Hooks Your Audience?

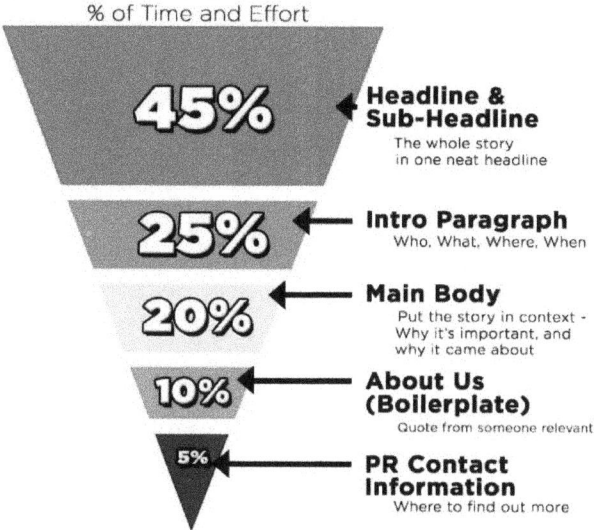

% of Time and Effort

45% → **Headline & Sub-Headline**
The whole story in one neat headline

25% → **Intro Paragraph**
Who, What, Where, When

20% → **Main Body**
Put the story in context - Why it's important, and why it came about

10% → **About Us (Boilerplate)**
Quote from someone relevant

5% → **PR Contact Information**
Where to find out more

© 2017 Brand You! Guide

11.
Distribute Your Release Online and in Person

Now that you've written your press release, you need to get it out to the media to get it published! You have the option to send the release out yourself, or use a press release distribution services to get it sent out digitally to thousands of media vehicles.

Build Your Media List

It can take hours to research each different media outlet you want to reach, and find the contact information for the right editor or journalist, whether locally or nationally. Most publications have a masthead or page that lists contact information for editors or staff writers. For print publications, contact the appropriate editor or writer – news, business, events. sports, food, books, community, fashion, etc. For TV and radio stations, you will probably need to contact the news desk. Most journalists are very busy in the afternoon getting ready for primetime news, so it's best to contact them in the morning.

Buy a Media List

You can purchase quality media lists from a number of sources. I have been very happy with media lists that I purchased from Easy Media List (www.EastMediaList.com) which came as a referral from my friend Irma Woodruff who is a public relations expert. For most markets, you can purchase a list of all media outlets in your target market for around $50. National lists can cost several hundred dollars.

Pitch Your Story to Your Select Media

Email your release to the relevant news editor or journalist, then follow up immediately with a phone call to pitch your story, and tell them that you just emailed them a release. As a general rule, you will get someone to check their email feed and identify your email and pull up your released. There is no guarantee that they will cover your story, but at least they will see it rather than have it buried in the stack without being seen.

Use a Press Release Distribution Service

To meet your objective of ranking in Google, you may wish to use an online press release service. Full service press release distribution can cost hundreds of dollars through large companies like PR Newswire or Business Wire. However, there are a number of companies that offer free or low cost distribution of your press release to a limited online audience. These are great resources, because it doesn't really matter if your release is picked up by anyone except Google! Online releases are often republished by aggregators, so your release may be picked up in strange places — you won't know until you see them on Google!

Here is an example of a page from a press release I distributed through 24-hour Press Release (www.24-7pressrelease.com/) several years ago, and the coverage report and sample clips of coverage it received. Today their entry-level package for digital distribution costs $49.

NEWS RELEASE

For Immediate Release

For More Information, contact Diane Huth, (210) 601-7852, or diane@BIOVIDEO.com.
Video at BIOVIDEO.com/experience

Father's Day Profile: How One Dad's Birth Experience Created a New Industry

Frustrated at filming his baby's first day of life, one first-time dad decided to create breathtaking videos of all new babies– for free – while still in the hospital

San Antonio, TX, June 11, 2013

In 2005, Carlos Villasenor and his wife Sylvia arrived at the hospital to give birth to their first child, Mariana. After 2 heartbreaking miscarriages, the couple was thrilled to finally bring their beautiful baby girl into the world, and the proud dad wanted to capture every priceless memory on film.

While the birth went without problem, Carlos' mission of filming the most special moments was rockier than expected. Everything seemed to go wrong for the anxious new dad.

"I was a nervous wreck, worrying about charging the camera, changing memory cards, and trying to preserve every priceless moment on film. The camera on the video camera ran down. That's when I discovered I had left the charging cable at home. Then the memory card filled up within hours, and I didn't have another one," he explained. When he decided to edit the clips into a movie as a gift for family and friends that Christmas, he realized that he wasn't in the film, as he had been behind the camera instead of beside his wife during many heartwarming moments. "I made up my mind then and there that I'd never have to choose between holding my wife's hand and holding the camera. No Dad should have to make that choice."

So the young newspaper executive became an entrepreneur, and founded BIOVIDEO to film and edit videos of a family's first day together at San Jose hospital in Monterrey Mexico the next year. The program was so popular with maternity patients that other hospitals requested the service, and soon BIOVIDEO movies were available to new parents in 90% of all the leading private hospitals in the key Mexican cities of Mexico City, Monterrey and Guadalajara.

A few years later, Carlos moved his family, then with 3 young daughters, to San Antonio to expand the BIOVIDEO vision to US families and hospitals.

(210) 601-7852   diane@BIOVIDEO.com

BIOVIDEO   MY LIFE ON VIDEO

This is an example of a report on the above press release distribution that shows it reached 182,876 people, was actually viewed by 1,106 people, was then sent by email to 225 people, and 11 people watched the attached video. You can see how the release was picked up word-for-word in most publications - which should be your goal.

Free or Low Cost Press Release Distribution Services

Companies may change their policies over time to eliminate the free release option, but at the time of writing, these companies (and many more) are currently offering free or low cost press release distribution. Please note that I have not used them all, and their coverage may be spotty at best:

- PR.com — http://www.pr.com/

- Online PR News — https://www.onlineprnews.com/

- PressReleaser.org — http://pressreleaser.org/

- Open PR — http://www.openpr.com/news/submit.html

- Google News — http://GoogleNewsSubmit.com/ currently $39

Getting a Story Published is the Best Way to Show Up in Google Search

Distributing a release online is one way to ensure you show up in Google search – something you can control or influence. But the best way to be found on Google is to be mentioned in any published newspaper, magazine or trade association article or news report.

As a general rule, smaller, local, niche or trade publications are starved for news and original content, and they may have just one or two writers. So your press release has a better chance of being picked up by a small outlet if it is well written and of interest to their audience base. While your goal may be just to rank in Google search, getting real life local press coverage is absolutely the most wonderful way to build your brand.

No story is too small if you want press coverage and a higher rank on Google. Write an article for your school paper, or submit a letter to the editor of a magazine or newspaper. Comment on blogs and include your name; perhaps ask to become a guest blogger, or start your own blog. Volunteer, be active at church or professional associations that create or receive media coverage. You may also get media coverage or mention if you participate in sporting events that regularly receive some kind of news coverage. So get involved and get noticed.

12.
6 Key Social Media Sites Every Job Seeker Needs to Master

I believe there are 6 key social media sites that you need to use to brand yourself professionally. While you may think of sites like Facebook, Twitter and Pinterest as fun social engagement tools to stay in touch with family and friends, they can become powerful assets in your career development and job search. Likewise, if used incorrectly, they can torpedo your career and prevent you from landing your dream job.

Read on to learn how to put these powerful branding tools to work to help you get hired.

6 Key Social Media Sites You Need Today

Key social media site
You can post content, ask questions, follow, comment, connect for research, search employees for jobs

Highlight your actions
Show photos of appropriate personal events, school or professional activities, follow and LIKE people and firms of interest, share professional content, quotes, images

Marketing & PR
Journalists and bloggers post all their content on Twitter, important in the marketing community, follow and like key content providers

Key social media site
Growing in popularity, often used for corporate content

Great source of images
And visual posts. Follow key industry trends and post insightful content on other sites, brand contests

Marketing & PR
Subscribe to channels of market leaders, potential employers, industry associations to get notices of new content, great for discussion during interviews

© 2016 Superhero Branding and Marketing, Inc

13.
LinkedIn – Your Number One Job Hunting Resource

One of the first things your prospective employers will do is to look at your LinkedIn page — and see what it says about you professionally. According to one study, 94% of recruiters and human resource (HR) professionals name LinkedIn as the essential source for recruiting. LinkedIn is where you'll build and promote your professional profile, job history, education, affiliations, and so much more. If you don't have a LinkedIn page yet, sign up today. If you have a page already, update it with current information — it will walk you step-by-step through many of the options available. And of course list your contact information, including email and phone number.

Why LinkedIn is your key job search platform:

- # of Active Job Listings on LinkedIn   **6.5 million jobs**
- # of LinkedIn users that identify as contractors   **4 million**
- % of recruiters that use LinkedIn to vet candidates   **94%**
- Increase in job views on LinkedIn compared   **5.7 X**
  to Facebook

Basic LinkedIn services are free, and a basic free account generally is adequate if you are employed. But if you are actively seeking a new job, you might consider upgrading to a Premium account which gives you access to hidden profiles and the ability to send InMail directly to any LinkedIn member even if you are not currently connected to them. LinkedIn has recently introduced the Career Plan, tailored for job seekers, at $29.99 per month. It may well be worth the investment if it helps you land your next job. LinkedIn is a powerful tool to network and reach out to potential employers or business colleagues you wouldn't be able to reach otherwise.

LinkedIn is a great networking and self-promotion tool, where colleagues can endorse you for specific skills, and you can show how savvy you are through the number of connections you have. But it can be much more than that. Today you can also post photos, comments, questions, blog posts, skills, presentations, white papers, and more. You can create an online portfolio on LinkedIn instantly viewable by everyone – for free. You can engage with other professionals by answering their questions or responding to and commenting on their posts and articles. This will make you stand out from other job candidates. LinkedIn should be your number one priority in your job search.

LinkedIn has perfected their site to the point where I suggest you build your LinkedIn profile BEFORE you create your résumé. LinkedIn will walk you step-by-step through every aspect of your career credentials, and prompt you if you are missing anything, such as employment dates or titles. If you complete your LinkedIn profile first, you have a great start on creating your powerful résumé later on.

Here is just a partial listing of features or products you can take advantage of to make your personal brand shine:

Create Your Profile - Your first step is to create a free account and build out your basic profile. Use your professional photo that you use on all your job search materials. A great photo is key, as recruiters actively view your photos for insights into your employability. You can add a background image if desired, as long as it doesn't detract from your profile photo.

Headline - Choose a headline that clearly states who you are and what you do. This is a key search tool for recruiters looking for qualified job candidates, so make sure your headline and description are filled with searchable keywords.

Contact and Personal Information - Ensure that a recruiter or hiring manager can find you and contact you quickly and effortlessly. Fill this section out completely. I suggest you use your permanent professional email address and not a school address. You can link social media pages here, and much more.

Education – You will be prompted to enter details of your education, step-by-step, and they will be arranged in the appropriate reverse chronological order – most recent fist, older information on the bottom. Easy as pie.

Employment – Again you will be prompted to fill in details of employment, which will be arranged in reverse chronological order. Use keywords, and focus on accomplishments rather than just a job description. A word about your LinkedIn employment profile and résumé: You must be rigorously honest and consistent — no cheating and no exaggeration. Make sure your LinkedIn profile mirrors your résumé. All this information is archived online for anyone to see, and any inconsistencies will pop up instantly. Your online résumé will become a public document that is cached online, so you must be totally honest and upfront about your information. You will learn how to create your powerful résumé in Book 2 of this series.

Build Your Connections – LinkedIn will ask you for access to your email accounts, and match your contacts to other LinkedIn members, and suggest that you connect via an invitation they will send on your behalf. Just click to invite, and you will start gaining connections quickly and easily.

Gaining Endorsements - You want people to endorse you for your skills, especially as you start out your career. The easiest way to get an endorsement is to endorse them first! Just review all your contacts and write a short but glowing endorsement about each of them — a sentence or two is enough — and submit in online. In return, the majority will give YOU an endorsement. And you don't even have to ask them for it!

Create Posts – These are quick messages of a timely nature, often with a call to action - notices about upcoming events or requests for information, invitations to apply for a job, etc. They can include images with insightful headlines, memes, quotes, etc. You can share posts from others that are relevant to your professional life. Here is where you will ask the LinkedIn community for introductions to key contacts at your desired company, or ask for information about a target employer or industry.

Post Articles – You can post longer thoughtful articles of professional interest, often several pages long, accompanied by an image. You can include links to photos or videos or additional information. These are evergreen posts, meaning they will be viewed for a long period of time. I have articles and posts from years ago that are still being seen and liked.

Jobs – The Jobs icon on the menu bar allows you to search companies and individuals anywhere. You can select a range of search criteria, including individual name, company name, industry, current employees, former employees, market or geography, job titles, education, experience level and much more. This is why you need a great headline loaded with keywords. Recruiters will search for keywords, and may find YOU with a well-written LinkedIn profile.

Messaging – You can send instant messages to anyone in your community quickly with a single click, and likewise receive messages from anyone in your network. You will also receive alerts about events – birthdays, job changes, work anniversaries, posts made, etc.

InMail – This is a premium service that requires a paid plan to allow you to message people outside your own network – such as potential employers. It also unmasks some senior executives whose contact is hidden on the regular platform. This can be a key reason to subscribe to a paid premium plan.

Groups – You can join and follow many different LinkedIn groups, which is important to expand your network and optimize your job search. Join your alumni groups, professional trade association groups, or groups that reflect a professional interest. You can use this platform to message members to help gain contacts or insights for your job search. Recruiters often check what groups you are following.

Learning Videos – LinkedIn has hundreds of informational videos, many created by members, that can provide a wealth of information. Check them out.

Slideshare – This is a forum which allows you to post PowerPoint presentations, infographics, white papers or other documents of useful professional information which you are willing to share freely with the online community. These presentations are evergreen, meaning they will be relevant forever or for a long time. A good Slideshare presentation may garner thousands of views over time, and can establish you as an expert.

Salaries – LinkedIn is a great source of information about salaries to help in your job search. They can provide a general range of salaries based on your desired job title. If you provide them with your current salary and company, they will tailor a market analysis which will be much more specific.

So Much More - There are many more tools available on LinkedIn, with new ones added every day. Go step-by-step to build your profile using this list, and you will soon have a powerful LinkedIn profile that will set you up for job search success.

If you'd like help polishing your LinkedIn profile, feel free to contact me at BrandYouGuide.com.

14.
Facebook – Show How You Invest Your Time and Energy

Half of all potential employers will look at your Facebook page as part of the screening process, according to *CareerBuilder*. It will tell them who you are as a person — what your interests are, how you spend your time, who you associate with, how you express yourself in writing, your political affiliation, whether or not you are married, or if you are a partier, a jock or a couch potato.

What are they going to find on YOUR Facebook page today?

Search through the last 3 months of your Facebook posts and evaluate yourself as an employer will. Are you family-oriented, or do you hang out with friends? Do you drink and go to nightclubs and party hard every weekend? Do you spend hours on end playing video games? What values do you express in your posts? Are many of your posts about alcohol, sex or laced with profanity or cynicism? Or do you engage in positive or altruistic activities such as volunteer work or church activities? Do you walk in charity events, belong to the Y, or participate in Ironman competitions? Do you care for and spend time with parents, family members, your spouse or children? Potential employers will look at your posts with these questions in mind to understand you as a person.

You should also stay clear of political posts and comments on your Facebook page. Half of all Americans belong to the other party, so you can't afford to offend them!

Employers are generally looking for a stable mature adult with some family responsibilities so they know you will take the job seriously and won't quit on a whim. Any potential employer will invest tens of thousands of dollars in training you for the job, and they want to feel comfortable that you are a reliable, serious employee who will fit into the company culture.

3 Steps to Manage Your Facebook Postings

1. Go through your own Facebook timeline and delete any photos or posts that will not look good to a potential employer. To remove objectionable posts, highlight the little down arrow on the top right corner of the post, and click "delete" or "hide from timeline."

2. If you are tagged in someone else's unflattering post, ask them to hide or delete the post in which you are tagged.

3. Actively start posting positive messages and images that a potential employer will appreciate. Post inspirational messages. Talk about positive things you are doing. Post about successes in school or work, or charity events you are involved in. Make posts that show your value system. Post about family members and business or community leaders you admire. Share positive stats, information, or images relating to your profession. But be authentic. Let your Facebook page sing your praises to a potential employer.

TIP — Google Might Find That Photo!
Beware of photos that show you in a less-than-desirable pose. Does your Facebook page show a photo of you partying drunk on Spring Break, or dressed provocatively, or making an obscene gesture? Google's spiders search through images on the Web, and they could pick up unflattering photos of you to post on Google Images! If they do, it might be very hard to make these go away. So be aware that everything that's on social media may be visible to a potential employer.

Create a Separate Professional Facebook Page

Have a professional Facebook page available for potential employers to easily find. If you aren't willing to have a single page that meets both your personal and professional needs, then you should consider making your current personal page private, and creating a separate public Facebook page in your full professional name that you will use on your résumé.

15.
Twitter - Follow Thought Leaders to Become One

Do you Tweet? Prospective employers may look at your Twitter feed and see what you're talking about. They're going to see if your posts are insightful or silly, if you follow thoughtful leaders and journalists or shallow Hollywood celebrities, and so much more. Use Twitter to showcase your skills and strengths, not to show weaknesses.

Use Twitter to Grow Professionally and Impress Prospective Employers

Most people think of using Twitter for fun, but it can play a very important role in your career. Most journalists use Twitter to post their stories and interact with followers. Follow a dozen or so important thought leaders in your desired industry, and comment insightfully every time they post a new story. You will go far in your own professional networking, and you will impress potential employers with your commitment to and knowledge of your field.

Twitter is Important for Marketers and Many Business Fields

You will need to have a Twitter account if you work in marketing, journalism, public relations, and many other fields. If you want to get a story published, you need to follow the key writers you wish to engage with through their Twitter feeds. For example, if you want to place a story in *Forbes*, follow the writers and editors who cover your industry or topics for *Forbes*. Start following them on Twitter, LIKE and SHARE their stories, and post insightful and favorable comments on every story. Soon you will be chatting with key writers like old friends, so when you want to place a story in *Forbes*, you have a colleague that you can easily contact.

16.
Register These Additional Social Media Pages

While LinkedIn, Facebook, and Twitter are the top social media sites you will need for your job search, you can use several other social media and digital tools for promoting your professional life. Take a few moments now to register these accounts in your same professional name so you have a consistent social media presence.

Pinterest

You should have a professional Pinterest page — it's not just for women and personal fun anymore. Create a professional account with boards that profile your professional heroes, give motivational quotes, state key insights about your profession, etc. LIKE each pin you post, then follow everyone whose pin you post, and they will probably follow you — allowing you to build your social media following. You can even link your Pinterest page directly to your Facebook page or Twitter account, and share pins directly to those social media sites.

Google+

I personally don't use Google+, but many business professionals do. The key benefits include immediate listing of your content on Google, and a higher Google ranking for your page and content than through organic search. If you register a YouTube page, you will automatically be assigned a Google+ page. To put it in perspective, there are more active Google+ accounts than Twitter accounts, so you understand the scale it offers. With the growing power of Google, I suggest that you register a Google+ page in your name now, even if you don't do anything with it right now. Or just duplicate your Facebook or LinkedIn posts on G+ using HootSuite.

YouTube

Communication today is shifting to video, so take the time now to register your own professional YouTube channel. You don't even need to post anything on your own channel today to benefit your job search. Simply subscribe to the channel of every company or brand you want to work for — and their competitors. For example, if you want to work for Procter and Gamble (P&G) on Pampers, subscribe to Pampers' YouTube Channel, and also to Huggies' and LUV's channels. Every time one of them posts a new video, you'll get an email alert so you can immediately watch the video. You can LIKE it, SHARE it, and post comments on the page that will be seen by Pampers' marketing team. You can send an email commenting on the new video to the recruiter or hiring manager at P&G that you want to connect with. At your upcoming job interview, you can say "I found your new Olympics video campaign was very motivational and right on target," or make an insightful comment about a competitor's campaign. Are you going to look sharp or what?

Even if you don't use your professional page now, you will have your name reserved for use in the future. Post your holiday vacation videos on a *personal* page; create and use your *professional* page for the many professional videos you will make as you evolve in your career.

Register New Social Media Pages as They Become Popular

Social media pages are free to claim and register today, so you might as well grab them while you can to secure them in your name. Why let somebody else take your name? Sometime in the next ten years, you may need these and other new social media sites. So register all your professional social media pages — including Instagram and Snap Chat and other new social media accounts as they become popular.

17.
Other Online Marketing Tools to Claim Now

While you're at it, you may want to secure a free Skype account for free video calls anywhere in the world. You can also buy Skype credits to call anyone internationally, regardless of their cellular carrier.

Other useful Skype features include Screen Sharing. With Screen Sharing, you can share your desktop with other Skype users so that they can see what you're working on, in real-time. There are also the usual functions like sending pictures, files, and even video messages.

I spend hours on Skype working with a graphic designer and my book editor sharing screens. And I review the financial P&Ls and worksheets of my marketing students using Skype so we can all collaborate instantly.

Due to its ubiquity, most companies also use Skype for video interviews. So don't miss out - register your free Skype account now.

You can also register for an easy-to-use free Mail Chimp account. Mail Chimp is an e-mail marketing platform where you can send e-mail campaigns to your contacts and other leads. It has many different templates available, in an easy-to-use interface. That way, you won't have to send out hundreds of emails one-by-one. Your campaigns will look like they were professionally done by a big media or ad agency.

Mail Chimp is free for the first 2,000 emails in your database, for unlimited email deliveries each month — that is a huge number of contacts. It also integrates with many other programs you will need in your professional life.

Eventbrite

You should register for a free EventBrite account at the same time, which will allow you to easily plan and promote events for free.

What sets Eventbrite apart from other event promotion platforms? A lot. With Eventbrite, you can plan and promote events and share them across all your social media platforms. You can manage your tickets and make promos too! All of these are done through their simple, intuitive website. They even have apps for Apple and Android as well. Plus you can integrate with Mail Chimp for marketing your events with widgets to post on websites and in emails.

With these social media tools, you will be well on your way to a powerful personal branding program using cutting edge digital techniques.

18.
Manage Your Social Media
Pages the Easy Way

A key to building your online presence is to have multiple social media pages. When I set up my Superhero Branding program, I spent hours searching and registering all the different social media sites I thought I might need in the future.

Then I learned that there's a much better way. I have found two companies, KnowEm.com and Namech_k.com, that will actually search all the social media sites and tell you if your name is available on each different page. It can save you hours of time.

knowem? Namech_k

Hootsuite™

HootSuite is a great free tool for managing all your social media accounts. You may think to yourself, "Oh I don't need that. I'm signed in to all my accounts anyway and can just copy paste everything quickly." Think again. HootSuite can post across all your linked social media accounts, with just 1 click of the mouse. Not only does it save you time, but it also makes you look professional: all your posts are standard across all your social media accounts — Facebook, Twitter, LinkedIn, Google+, WordPress, Instagram and YouTube. You can also quickly and easily schedule posts, edit image previews, as well as shorten links using their handy tools.

The basic membership is free, and there is a small monthly fee for multiple users on one account for businesses. It's easy to learn, and there are a lot of tutorials and a dedicated community that responds to user inquiries. This is an effective way to be professionally active in social media without driving yourself crazy!

19.
Create Your Own Website for Powerful Personal Branding

Now is the time to register your own professional name as a domain name before anyone else does. I bought www.DianeHuth.com more than a decade ago. I don't do anything with it because I'm busy with other things and have it redirected to one of my business websites, but I would never give it up so someone else could take it.

I strongly recommend you use GoDaddy for all your domain and web services — I have had nothing but the most outstanding customer service from them 24/7 by knowledgeable techs who live in the United States! They are the only web domain and web services company you ever will need. It'll cost you around $20 a year to own your domain name. They often offer discounts for services — right now they are offering a promotion for $1.00 for a new annual domain registration, $1.00 per month Website Builder and $3.99 per month web hosting with professional emails.

I suggest you build a small 1- to 3-page professional website to serve as a digital résumé and portfolio. Showcase your skills, projects you have done, your business philosophy and more. The GoDaddy Website Builder is very easy and intuitive to use, and you can build a professional and attractive website in just a few hours. Then it just takes minutes to update it at no additional cost. If you need help building your site, contact us at Diane@BrandYouGuide.com.

20.
Step-by-Step Guide to Build Your Own Website in 4 Hours or Less

Here's a quick tutorial on building your personal website using GoDaddy's intuitive platform. It will show you how I built a website for my brother's company, Vespa Solutions:

1. Register an account with GoDaddy.com.

2. Verify the account through your e-mail, and sign in to GoDaddy.com.

3. Before you can proceed with the Website Builder, you have to buy your own domain first. To do this, go to domain search and enter the name that you want for your potential website.

4. The domain search results will appear. GoDaddy will also give suggestions if your preferred domain is already taken.

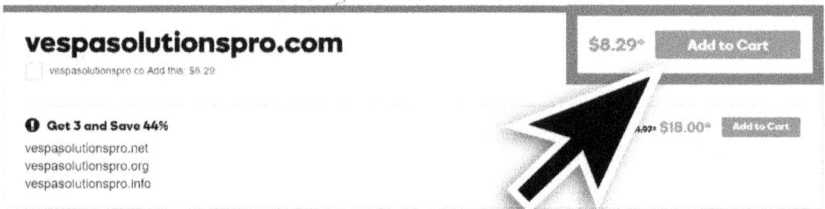

5. Choose your domain, then click "Select." Then, "Proceed to Checkout" to purchase your domain. Specify the number of years you want to purchase (they will default it to 5 years if you don't select the 1 year option:

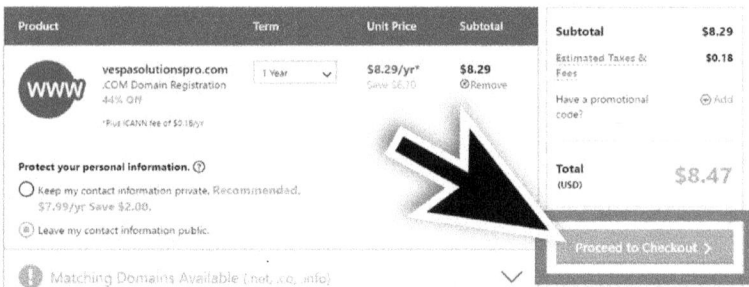

TIP – Register multiple domain names to protect your name

Register other domains which are similar in name and by nature to your business. Why? Because hijackers may register similar domains and mislead your customers, thereby stealing your business. For example: Facedook, Facbook, and many more minor misspelled links all redirect back to Facebook.com.

6. Now it's time to start building your website! In the Home Page, there's an option to Build a Website: Start for Free! Click on the button to continue.

Build a new website

Build

7. There are many different Website Builder options to choose from. Choose the plan that best suits your needs. Check out the different benefits below:

		Most Popular	eCommerce
Personal	**Business**	**Business Plus**	**Online Store**
For sharing your passion online	For businesses just starting out	For businesses looking for more customers	For businesses that want to sell products online
Start for Free	Start for Free	Start for Free	Start for Free
No credit card required. Try it free for one month. Then $5.99/mo ($71.88/yr) after	No credit card required. Try it free for one month. Then $9.99/mo ($119.88/yr) after	No credit card required. Try it free for one month. Then $14.99/mo ($179.88/yr) after.	No credit card required. Try it free for one month. Then $29.99/mo ($359.88/yr) after.
Responsive mobile design	Responsive mobile design	Responsive mobile design	Responsive mobile design
Website hosting	Website hosting	Website hosting	Website hosting
24/7 support	24/7 support	24/7 support	24/7 support
	PayPal integration	PayPal integration	PayPal integration
	Security (SSL)	Security (SSL)	Security (SSL)
	Search Engine Optimization (SEO)	Search Engine Optimization (SEO)	Search Engine Optimization (SEO)
		Email Marketing	Email Marketing
		Social Media Integration	Social Media Integration
		Globally-Optimized Speed	Globally-Optimized S
			Built-in shopping ca checkout

Let's Chat
Click here

55

8. Fill in the blanks that best identify your site, business, or service.

What's your site about?

Pick a topic so we can tailor your site with professional pictures to get started.

Gym, Real Estate, Bakery

What do we call your site?

You know, the name of your business, event or whomever or whatever the site's all about

9. GoDaddy will create a theme that matches your business. If you don't like it, don't worry, you can always change it! There are many themes to choose from.

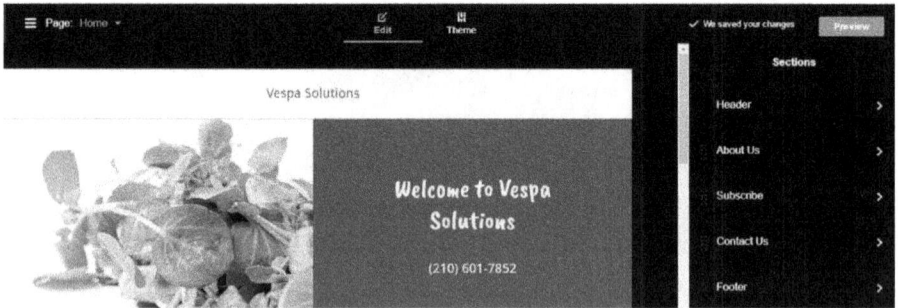

From here, feel free to customize your website. The right side lists the *Sections,* or the Main parts of your website. You can edit the writeup, and add links too.

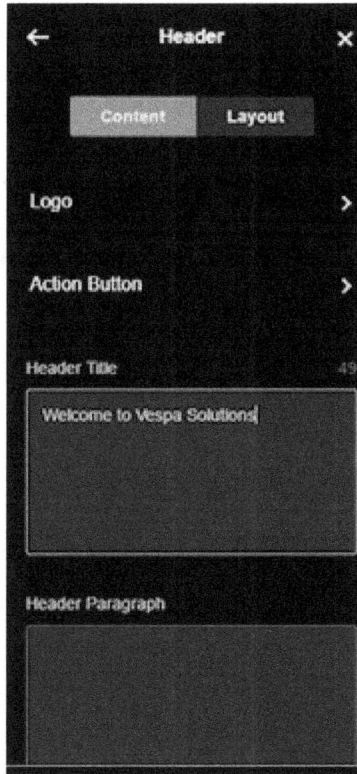

The main screen contains all the visual elements. You can add images, edit the text, and it'll appear exactly as you see it on screen.

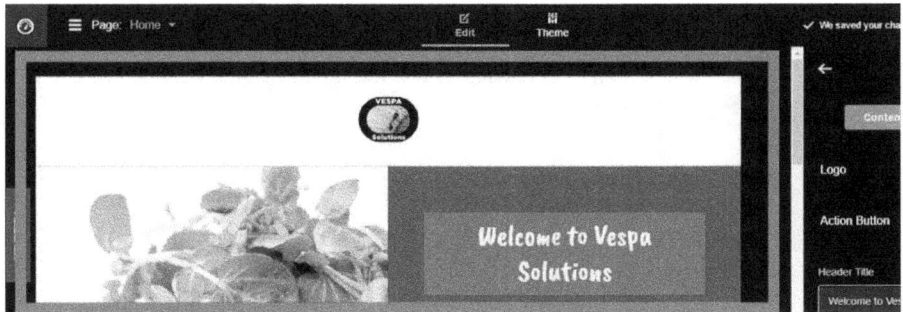

10. Once you are satisfied with the changes you've made, click "Preview" on the upper right-hand corner of the site. You'll see the web and mobile previews of your site. Go back and continue editing until you are happy with the results. Then, click on "Publish".

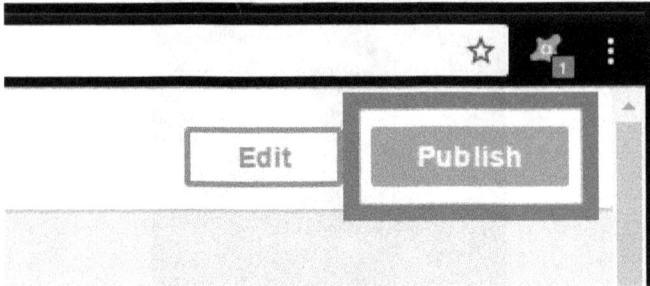

Congratulations! You have created your website with Go Daddy's Website Builder, no coding required!

21.
Start Your Own Consulting Company

I believe that every working professional with more than 5 years of experience should have your own consulting company, to serve as credentials when unemployed or looking or a job. It's the best Plan B out there for your career.

You don't have to do anything other than print business cards and build a small website that you are planning to do anyway, right?

You don't need to file for an LLC or incorporate if you use your own name and work as a sole proprietor .

You may want to apply for a Fictitious Name for your business if you choose a name other than your own name. Check out the page on Corporations on your local state Secretary of State webpage for rules on sole proprietorships and taxation as these vary state-to-state.

You can also choose to form a corporation (select the S-corp option) or an LLC (Limited Liability Corporation), but that involves filing fees of several hundred dollars, renewal filings, annual reports and more. Unless you start generating a substantial income through the business, or are at risk of personal liability for your professional actions, it probably isn't worth the expense and hassle, when a sole proprietorship would work just as well. Contact your CPA or attorney for guidance is setting up your business structure.

One important benefit is that, as a consultant, you can interface with potential employers as a professional peer rather than as a job applicant. As a consultant, you are able to reach out to the hiring manager, while as a job seeker, the organization tries to limit contact through the HR department. Make a plastic name tag with your name, and business name and functional interests, and get networking!

As a consultant, you will find yourself in a much more powerful position while interacting with potential employers or clients. It's so easy to ask for an appointment to learn about their business to see if there is some way you could help them reach their goals. A consulting position will frequently turn into a full-time job offer. Don't worry – if you find your dream job, you can always put your consulting business on a back burner or subcontract work to a trusted freelancer while you focus your energies on your new job. But it's reassuring to know it is always there as a fallback when you suddenly need it.

And there are great tax benefits for working out of a home office. You can generally deduct a portion of your rent or mortgage, utilities, phone and internet, home cleaning and gardening services, and more. If you legitimately call on customers during a trip, you can deduct part of travel costs. You just have to make more money than your deductions to be able to benefit fully from the home office expense deductions.

Check with the IRS (IRS.gov) or your CPA to learn tax implications based on your business structure, and what you can and can't deduct for business and home office expenses.

22.
Monitor Your Credit Report

Today, about 35% of companies use your credit report to find out how responsible you are and to judge your character. When you sign the job application, you give the employer permission to access personal information, which includes your credit report.

Credit scores range from a low of 300 to a high of 850, with an average of around 660. If you have a poor or average credit score, work to improve it now by paying down outstanding balances, and ensuring you pay minimum balances on time.

If you are new to the work market, you may not have a credit rating. In this case, apply for 3 or 4 credit cards (Master Card, Visa, retail cards, gas cards, etc.). Use each of these at least once a month, and pay them off promptly each month. This will help build a high credit score quickly.

Several major credit cards (including Capital One, Chase and Bank of America) offer free credit reports as a feature of their card app. Check your credit score monthly to track your credit-building progress.

23.
Manage Your Passwords
and Login Information

You will need to keep track of all your domain names and social media pages, or the constantly changing passwords will drive you crazy. I create a spreadsheet and record all my domain names, account numbers, social media pages, login email addresses, passwords, date of last update and more. You might even want to keep it in a Cloud drive to access from anywhere when you are away from your primary computer. This is in addition to my Password Manager app below.

I recommend you use a Password Manager program to keep track of all your passwords and log in information for all your accounts. I use Dashlane with an annual premium subscription costing around $40 per year. It automatically records each domain and account, and the login information, and then syncs across all platforms. According to *PC World*, the top ranked password managers include Dashlane, Sticky Password and Last Pass at the time this book was written. I suggest you do a Google search for "Best Password Managers" to select one that meets your needs.

Create Easy-to-Remember Passwords

You will be required to update your password frequently for many social media accounts. Instead of creating new passwords each time, you can change these by adding a progressive letter behind your standard password — which is much easier to remember. Example — Pass13*a, Pass13*b, Pass13*c, etc.

I tend to create an 8-digit password with a combination of caps, low case letters, numbers and special characters so it will work on the vast majority of sites. Then I just change the last character sequentially from A up to Z so the password is easy to remember and recover.

24.
Monitor and Track Your
Social Media Brand Presence

Monitoring, tracking and updating your social media presence is an ongoing responsibility. Set aside a block of time each week or month to update your LinkedIn page and monitor all of your social media accounts. This is an ongoing responsibility — to monitor, track and enhance your social media presence.

Google Yourself Monthly

Make yourself a calendar alert for once a month to conduct a Google search of your own name. Take a screen shot of the home page and any other pages you appear on; date it and keep it in a file. Over time you will be able to see changes as your brand presence increases.

Set Google Alerts

Here's a handy secret tool you may not know about. Go to Google Alerts and set up a free account to track anything published about yourself, your industry, your school or university, potential employers, even topics you are interested in. You can register up to 10 free names, keywords, or domain names. You will receive an email whenever your listed name or keyword is mentioned in any media or online post anywhere. So if you've sent those press releases and one gets picked up in an online blog anywhere in the country, you will learn about it instantly! Armed with this hot-off-the-presses information, you can proactively reach out to prospective employers and mentors immediately, mentioning the content of the news story, so they know you are really connected, alert, and on the cutting edge — just the kind of employee they are looking for!

25.
Select Your Professional Name —
and Stick with it Forever

You need to select the professional name that you'll use forever. Your professional name will appear on your résumé, LinkedIn page, personal or professional website, permanent email address, business cards, diplomas, transcripts, and more.

When you did your Google search, how many people were listed with the same name as yours? If just one or two, then you don't have a problem — other than having a very strange or unusual name!

Most likely, there were dozens of people with the same name. So you need to create your permanent name to be as distinctive yet professional as possible to stand out in social media and avoid confusion with someone with a similar name.

Most names are fairly common, so you will probably want to add a middle initial or middle name — which will allow you to stand out. Some people don't have a middle name. If that is the case, just make one up — you get to choose! How fun! But make up one that you will like, because you will be stuck with it for a long time. You could choose an unusual middle initial — Q, X, Y and Z are all good — that will probably be unique as well.

You should also avoid fun or frivolous nicknames that might not be considered adequately professional. This is not the time to add your nickname of Bambi, Baby, Bonzo or Rocketman — leave those nicknames for close friends and family only and for your personal email.

For Women Only — Should You Use Your Maiden or Married Name?

If you are an unmarried woman, you should use your first, middle and last name. When you marry, I suggest that you replace your middle name with your maiden name, and then add your husband's name as your last name. For example, my maiden name was Diane Margaret Clauss, but when I married I dropped Margaret and added Huth — so my name now is Diane Clauss Huth.

When I divorced, I decided not to change my name back to my maiden name, because by that time I had established it as my professional name and it's my son's last name. However, if I had decided to drop my ex-husband's last name, most people would have been able to find me through my maiden name which I had kept as part of my legal married name.

Recommendations for Managing Married and Maiden Names

- **If you are young and plan to have children**, it will be easier on everyone involved if you adopt your husband's last name. Otherwise, your children's last names will be different from your name, which is very confusing to everyone, especially teachers and administrators. Plus, you will receive letters and Christmas cards addressed to Mr. and Mrs., and it just becomes a hassle. The wife of a cousin of mine refused to take his last name, and she spent decades scolding everyone about the Mr. & Mrs. issue, which only served to alienate everyone involved. It was a waste of time, effort and goodwill.

- **If you are a mature professional and you already have children**, you might want to keep your married name if you divorce. It will be much easier on everyone involved, and much simpler for the kids. Your professional name is your brand equity, and it is risky to change your personal branding unless absolutely necessary.

- **If your ex was Attila the Hun** and you absolutely hate him and his name, then by all means change it back to your maiden name. But beware that it will take time and effort to make the change to government documents, passports, drivers' licenses, diplomas and transcripts, social media pages, medical insurance, ID cards, mortgages, banks, and more.

- **Avoid hyphenating your husband's name** after your last name. A few years ago, it was popular for Mary Ellen Jones to become Mary Ellen Jones-Smith when she married Mr. Smith. But that just doesn't work for many government and industry online forms. For example, when traveling internationally, the customs agents will look at your last name only, so you will be registered as Smith or Jones and not Jones-Smith, which will drive computers crazy and may not match your passport. In addition, your hyphenated last name may be too long for certain forms or computer applications and you might end up being listed as Mary Ellen Jones-Sm. That doesn't work well either.

- **All this is easy to do** — just declare your new married name when you fill out the marriage certificate and send in your change of name to Social Security. Same thing when you get a divorce — just declare what your name will be. No need to go to court to make a name change or do any special legal filing. Ask an attorney if you have any questions or doubts of a challenging situation.

Now is the time to select and adopt a distinctive professional name and apply it consistently throughout your job search & professional life. Women, decide your long-term naming strategy now, and stick with it.

26.
Harness Powerful Email Tools
for Your Job Search

Create a Professional Gmail Account

A professional email address in your professional name is crucial for your personal branding. According to the website *BeHiring.com*, using an unprofessional email address will cause you to be rejected 76% of the time!

Not using Gmail yet? I strongly suggest that you create a Gmail account for your professional name. Gmail provides you with a wide range of apps and add-ons that will make your job search so much easier and efficient.

Hopefully, you can get your professional name@gmail.com account without a problem. But if it is already taken, try using hyphens or periods to create your unique Gmail account.

For example, my professional email account is DianeHuth@gmail.com. But if it wasn't available, I could have tried one of these alternative addresses: Diane.Huth or Diane.C.Huth, or Diane-Huth or even DianeHuthTX. With email addresses, caps and low case letters are interchangeable — it doesn't matter which you use. So you can use caps in promoting or listing your email address for good readability and to correspond to your name visually. The key is to keep the name integrity to ensure your email address is easily memorable and identifiable as being you.

TIP — Gmail is Wonderful!

You'll use Gmail for everything. It links to the whole Google ecosystem, so claim your name before someone else does. For older professionals, legacy email accounts like AOL, Yahoo, and People PC are considered old fashioned and may indicate that you are older and/or not up to date with your social media skills. Similarly, avoid using email addresses from your internet or cable company. When you change service or move, you may have to give up that address, which will seriously hamper your personal branding program.

If you set up your own website and domain name, you may be able to use a permanent email address like diane@dianehuth.com. For $50 a year, Gmail can also administer your email account so you can access all the other great marketing tools that integrate with the Google platform.

Create a Visual Signature Stamp

As you communicate with potential employers — and for the rest of your life — you need a professional graphic signature. Google has a free app called WiseStamp (https://Webapp.wisestamp.com/) that will create a signature as a picture that looks like this:

Diane Huth
Marketing Meister, Superhero Branding
(210) 601-7852 || Diane@SuperheroBranding.com ||
https://www.SuperheroBranding.com || Skype: diane.huth

It can feature your picture, email, phone, website, social media pages, and more. For less than $50 per year, you can upgrade to a pro account with multiple signatures customized to different email accounts and extra add-ons.

So instead of just typing your name and contact info when you are corresponding with a potential employer, you can brand yourself with a visual WiseStamp signature.

Set Up Email Tracking

Since you will be using email to reach prospective employers, you can benefit from setting up Email Tracking to know who and when someone opened your emails. A number of different services offer detailed tracking for your Gmail account, notifying you when someone opens your email, how many times it is opened, for how long it is open, and if it is forwarded and to whom. A tracking program ranges from free for a limited number of emails per day to unlimited emails for around $10 per month. *Computer World* in 2015 rated Bananatag, Boomerang, Mail2Cloud, MailTrack, Sidekick and YesWare as the best mail tracking programs.

27.
Master Correct Grammar and Spelling

In everything you do in your professional branding, you must be rigorous about grammar and spelling. There is no room for typos, misspelling, incorrect word usage, profanity, poor formatting, run-on sentences, or sloppy or unprofessional presentation.

According to *CareerBuilder.com*, 61% of recruiters will reject your résumé if it contains a single typo. And 43% of hiring managers will do the same thing, according to Adecco, a leading employment agency.

If I see a résumé, cover letter or LinkedIn profile that has a typo, bad grammar, or misspelling, I think that the candidate is not good enough to work for me. I immediately discard that résumé or application and go on to the next candidate. If something as important as your job-hunting materials aren't perfect, and if you don't carefully proofread, and you can't get the spelling and grammar right, I expect your work to be equally sloppy and unprofessional. I won't spend time teaching you how to spell or write as an employee. You have to get it right always.

Run All Communication Through a Spelling and Grammar Checker

Microsoft Word makes it incredibly simple to check your documents for errors, typos and bad grammar. It should automatically underscore in red any misspellings and in blue any questionable word choice.. But just in case, run a spelling and grammar check when you finish drafting a document of any kind, including a preliminary draft of an email before you copy it into your word processing program. In the top menu bar, click Review, then Spelling & Grammar and it will take you through every questionable item in the document for you to accept or change. Make a habit of checking all key documents before sending them. It can make the difference between getting the job or getting rejected – it is that important.

Tools for Improving Your Communication

If you don't have perfect English grammar and spelling, work on it immediately, as it will be a key barrier to getting a good job. If you are in school, you may be able to get a tutor from Career Services.

Always have your résumé and cover letter template reviewed by one or more people with great grammar.

Also avoid industry jargon and abbreviations whenever possible to ensure all recipients can understand what you are trying to say.

The easiest way to actively improve your grammar and word choice is to download and practice with any of dozens of great mobile apps that will train you on correct grammar. Here is a short list of some highly-recommended mobile apps that are free or inexpensive: Grammaropolis Complete, English Grammar Book, Grammar Up, Grammar Girl App, Grammar Phone, Grammar Police, Grammar Guru, Grammar App, and Practice English Grammar.

In addition, there is an app — Grammarly.com — that will check all of your emails before you send them. It works on both your emails and Word documents, and will send you a weekly report of key errors you tend to make to help you correct your grammar.

Now that you've established your digital and online presence, you are one step closer to finding your dream job.

28.
Next Step - Start Collecting All Your Job Hunting Tools

If you've gotten this far, then you have learned all the secrets to harnessing powerful online tools and resources to build your personal brand.

Your job search is a process, and not a particularly fast or easy one. You are at the beginning of the process.

Next you need to gather and prepare all the tools and resources you will need when you start to apply for a job.

Check out an excerpt from Book 2 – BRAND YOU To Build a Powerful Résumé and Job Hunting Tools… at the end of this book.

1	Master Your Social Media
2	Build A Powerful Résumé and Job Hunting Tools
3	Find And Monetize Internships
4	Become A Master Networker
5	Find, Apply For And Get The Interview
6	Master The Interview
7	Negotiate The Best Possible Offer

RESOURCES TO HELP YOU ON
THE PATH TO SUCCESS

Brand You Guide — www.BrandYouGuide.com
Here you will find free templates, checklists, examples, resources, and so much more. You can take advantage of our low-cost services to write or enhance your résumé, build your LinkedIn page, create an effective cover letter, write a press release, create your business card and visual branding, build your website, or benefit from one-on-one coaching. Register to receive our newsletter or subscribe to our blog. Use coupon code BU25 to receive a 25% discount off your first purchase.

Social and Digital Media Sites
Claim you name by registering for a free account at all these free social media and digital branding sites immediately. You don't need to build out a page right now, but make sure you secure you professional name before someone else claims it:

- LinkedIn
- YouTube
- Instagram

- Google+
- SWITCH app
- SnapChat

- Twitter
- JobR app

- Pinterest
- JobCase

Tools to Manage Your Online Presence
These sites can help manage your online presence and professional reputation:

- Godaddy
- EventBrite
- Hootsuite

- Skype
- Knowem
- Dashlane

- MailChimp
- Namech_k
- Google Alert

Email Management Tools and Tracking Services
Learn when someone opens your email by using one of these services that were the top ranked by *Computer World* in 2015:

- Gmail
- Boomerang
- Sidekick

- Wisestamp
- Mail2Cloud
- YesWare

- Bananatag
- MailTrack

Low Cost Press Release Distribution Sites
The largest and most prestigious press release sites include PR Newswire and Business Wire, but their services can be expensive. I have had great success with 24HourPressRelease.com for $49.

To receive free or inexpensive press release distribution, try some of these sites:

- Google News — http://Googlenewssubmit.com/ currently $19
- PR.com — http://www.pr.com/
- Online PR News — https://www.onlineprnews.com/
- PressReleaser.org — http://pressreleaser.org/
- Open PR — http://www.openpr.com/news/submit.html

BIBLIOGRAPHY, SOURCES, CITATIONS, OPINIONS AND MORE

All opinions and insights presented in this book are my own unless attributed otherwise.

The workplace today is gender-neutral, so I refer to people as *"he"* or *"she"*, and no meaning should be attributed to the pronoun choice.

In writing this book, I did not consult, read or research any other books about this topic. I relied on my own experience garnered over more than 3 decades in the business world, having interviewed hundreds of candidates, and employing many dozens of people.

I did, however, conduct extensive online research on specific topics and gained valuable insights on the most current job statistics and market trends.

In today's digital world, information is openly shared across multimedia platforms, and an enormous amount of information is freely available through Google and other search engines. I found that the majority of relevant information was made available by companies engaged in the job search and recruiting industry, via their websites, blogs and white papers. Few provided dates of publication or author attribution. In this fluid environment, many documents cited each other, so identifying original sources was sometimes a challenge.

Here are some key sources of information I found of value in learning about the digital marketing tools which can benefit any job seeker:

Works Cited

"50 Job Search Statistics Successful Job Seekers Need To Know" *Julliengordon.com*, 11 Feb. 2013

"50 HR and Recruiting Statistics For 2016" - *glassdoor.com*/ b2b-Assets

Adler, Lou. "This Single Job Hunting Statistic Will Blow Your Mind" - *LinkedIn.com*, The Adler Group, 28 June 2016

"Average Salaries by Job and U.S. Location" - *Simply Hired.com*

"Career Statistics:" - *Experience.com*

"Official LinkedIn Blog." *LinkedIn.com*

Sportelli, Natalie. "Congrats On Graduating, Class of 2016! Here's What You Need to Know About the Real World", *Forbes.com*, 4 May 2016

Sullivan, Dr. John. "Why You Can't Get A Job … Recruiting Explained By the Numbers" - *www.eremedia.com*, 20 May 2013

"The Class of 2015 - Economic Policy Institute." *Epi.org*, Economic Policy Institute

"The Ultimate List of Hiring Statistics - LinkedIn." *LinkedIn.com*

Smith, Craig. "17 Interesting LinkedIn Job Statistics." www.expandedramblings.com, 24 March 2017

"5 Surprising Numbers from Uber's Driver Data Report." *Fortune.com*. 22 Jan. 2015

Modern Language Association 8th edition formatting by BibMe.org.

ACKNOWLEGEMENTS

THANKS TO MY EDITORS

Deep thanks go out to three wonderful friends who took their time to painstakingly read, edit and suggest revisions to the manuscript:

- Brook Carey, career coach, founder of Executeam SW Business Consulting, and franchising guru, Schertz TX
- Carla Schworer, fellow T-Bird alumni and non-profit leader of Las Vegas NV
- Emily Groenner, University Business Communication Instructor and Career Counselor, St. Cloud MN
- Miguel Castriciones from the Philippines for the layout and editing

IMAGE LICENSES

Most images used in this book were licensed from Dreamstime.com, or are proprietary images created especially for this book. Logos of recommended sites were sourced online from the respective sites. If you feel any images were used inappropriately or without permission, please contact me immediately at Diane@BrandYouGuide.com so they can be removed.

MEET THE AUTHOR

I'm Diane Huth, and I love helping other people achieve their goals.

I'm a branding and marketing expert, a university professor of marketing, and I'm known as the Accidental Career Coach.

I've worked in marketing forever (more than 30 years — yikes!) and I have loved at least 95% of everything I've done. I've run larger marketing departments for companies like Johnson & Johnson and Mission Foods, and worked in smaller entrepreneurial companies like Skinny Snacks and Biovideo.

I've screened thousands of résumés, interviewed hundreds of job candidates, hired scores of employees, and have mentored at least thirty college interns.

I am currently the CMO (Chief Marketing Officer) for Biovideo, a company that films the most heartwarming moments of a baby's first day, and transforms the images into a breathtaking video that we give to new parents at their baby's birth. So my day job lets me gift happiness all day long! Check it out at www.Biovideo.com or our Facebook Page at www.facebook.com/MyBiovideo.

For more than ten years I've been a Senior Innovation Strategist for Prodigy Works, creating breakthrough new product and innovation programs for leading national brands and companies.

Recently, I started teaching marketing and branding to college students at 2 different universities in my spare time, and I was shocked to learn how unprepared they were for their upcoming job search. These students had just spent 4 years of their young lives, and often $100,000 or more on college tuition, and they had no idea how to find a job when they graduated. So I wrote this book to help them — and you — find and land your dream job.

I currently teach part time at Texas A&M University and The University of the Incarnate Word, both in San Antonio, and I thank my great students for letting me try out and fine tune the content of this book.

As a result of the response to this book, I am now working on my second book, to be titled **Re-BRAND YOU To Re-INVENT Your Career**. It will help baby boomers who are out of work, stuck in a dead-end job, or fearful of losing their job to find meaningful, enjoyable and profitable employment as long as they wish to work. This second book will come out in the fall of 2017.

Contact me at Diane@BrandYouGuide.com or visit my website at www.BrandYouGuide.com. And look for me on Facebook and Pinterest!

Continue to read more for your career success.
Visit my Amazon page at http://goo.gl/vapDVW to buy the original 33-chapter book BRAND YOU! To Land Your Dream Job, or Book 2 in the mini e-book series.

Buy Your Book Today

✓ Paperback
✓ Kindle
✓ Workbook
✓ E-Books
✓ English & Spanish

www.goo.gl/vapDVW.com

If you've found this book helpful, please leave a short but sweet 5-star rave review!

I will very much appreciate it! It DOES matter a lot!

☆☆☆☆☆
―――――――――――

Keep reading for an excerpt of eBook 2!

Excerpt from
Book 2
BRAND YOU!
Build a Powerful Résumé
and Job Hunting Tools
To Land Your Dream Job

1.
Understand Who Makes the Hiring Decision

Companies don't really hire people; people do. One particular person will recommend you for a certain job, and one person has the responsibility or clout to decide if he wants you on the team. While there may be several people on the interview panel, and you will deal with an HR (Human Resources) manager who will make you the actual offer and negotiate your employment, they are not the decision-makers. Your future boss is the decision maker.

Understand the dynamics of the job decision-making process, and reach out to the key people who will make or break your employment.

Three Different Job Targets to Reach and Influence

You have 3 different job targets when you're looking for a job:

1. The person who's going to pay you; that's your future boss.

2. The person who influences your future boss; that's his boss, other colleagues in the department, people he knows, maybe the HR manager, professional colleagues etc.

3. Your supporters or mentors who take you under their wing and help you get introduced to the other people above.

Hopefully you have found your passion and know what you want to do professionally. Next you need to figure out the people who are going to get you there.

2.
Find and Recruit Mentors

You need at least one mentor who is skilled at business or in your career field and will take the time and interest to guide you and help you find your dream job.

Your mentor will be someone you really connect with on a personal or professional level. It can be a more senior person in your field, a company executive, a personal family friend, a relative, or even someone you meet on another job or volunteer work.

Your mentor should help you learn how to navigate the business world or your job field and cut through the red tape by introducing you to influential people in the hiring process.

You generally have to seek out a mentor. It's okay to just flat out ask someone to become your mentor — they probably will be deeply honored or flattered that you look up to them in this manner.

You should aim for perhaps 3 or 4 active mentors to guide you in your career. You won't be in touch with them on a daily or weekly basis, but you should reach out to each of them at least once a month, by phone or by email to help you keep on track and upbeat during a difficult job search.

Remember, mentor relationships are long-term, so once you find your job, call and tell them all about it. They will appreciate knowing about your success and will likely be ready and willing to help you on your next journey in your career.

➜ **TAKEAWAY** — Your mentors should actively give valuable insight, build your morale, provide unique points of view, and help you connect with others in your job search. Seek out several mentors and listen to what they have to say. Their outside perspective is very valuable.

3.
Line Up Your Personal and Professional References

Every employer is going to ask for references, so be prepared with a list of both personal and professional references before an employer asks for them. They will include your mentors, plus current and former employers, colleagues, vendors, customers, professors, colleagues from organizations you volunteer with. Select people who will write and say glowing things about you. Before you actively start your job search, call or talk with each of your mentors and ask if they will be willing to serve as a reference for you.

After your mentors say "Yes" to serving as a reference, make sure you have their contact information, which includes name, title, phone number, email and physical address. Create a nicely-formatted Word document with your contact information in the header or footer, and title it "References for <your name>." List each reference with contact information, and a brief one-sentence description of how you know or have worked with each person. Examples of suitable descriptions include:

- *Served on the Board of the AMA chapter together from 2014-2016*

- *Direct supervisor at XYZ Corporation; can attest to my team work skills and attention to detail*

- *Ad agency account executive; worked together on the XYZ account*

- *Youth Ministry Pastor of XYZ church; worked together to host the summer Vacation Bible Camp in 2015*

- *Professor of Marketing for 3 courses from 2015-2016; can speak to my work ethic and dedication to my passion for marketing*

- *Customer from 2010 - 2013; provided accounting services to his family-run landscaping business*

- *Business executive, longtime family friend; familiar with personal background and values*

Take several copies of this list of references to your job interview. If the company seems interested, leave one copy with the HR director. Keep one handy to use in filling out the Job Application, which they will probably ask you to complete, even though they have your detailed résumé.

Save the file in both Word and PDF format, so you can forward it to your HR contact with a follow-up email to thank them for your interview.

TIP — Shortcut to Filling Out the Job Application Form

Even through you may have already filled out an online application, HR will undoubtedly ask you to fill out a long and tedious hard copy application form during an in-person interview. What they really need is your signature giving them the legal right to contact former employers for references and to perform credit and criminal background searches. Shortcut the application by filling out just the contact information, Social Security number (make sure you have it memorized), anything that's NOT on your résumé or list of references, and signing and dating the application. Write in pen *"See attached résumé"* on all sections covered by your résumé. Then attach your résumé and list of references to the application with a paperclip (which you will bring in your briefcase) and hand it in to HR. It will look much better than trying to hand-write lots of information into too-tiny spaces, and your application will be clean and neat. Five minutes and you're done!

Let Each Reference Know to Expect a Call — And Coach Them on a Suggested Response

After sharing the list of references with a prospective employer, call each listed reference and let them know that they may receive a call asking for a reference. Tell them something like, *"I just applied for a job at XYZ corporation working in social media marketing for their automobile insurance division, and I listed you as a reference. Hopefully, you will get a phone call. If you do hear from them, I'd really appreciate it if you mentioned what a good job we did together on the Jones account last year and how we grew sales by 27%."*

You don't want them to just say, *"Yeah, she worked for me — I don't remember when."* You can benefit from reminding them of dates, stats accomplishments, and specifics that they can mention so their talking points will be fresh on their minds.

Lastly, ask them to give you a quick call if they DO get contacted by HR to let you know specific questions they asked, if they appeared to have any concerns or interest, and what your reference said about you. It will help you gauge how likely you are to get an offer.

TIP — Understand What Former Employers May and May Not Say About You

In today's litigious society, employers are hesitant to say too much or too little about you for fear of being sued. Each state has a different law about what can and cannot be disclosed in response to a request for employment verification, from almost nothing to a great deal of information — some of which you may not want revealed. If a prospective employer calls an HR department, the information they will receive is limited. The most they might receive is confirmation of:

- Whether or not you were ever employed by the company

- Your title or position

- Your dates of employment

- Your compensation level — confirmation of what you stated you earned

- Whether or not you are eligible to be rehired — it's the legal way to find out if you were fired or left in bad standing

➜ TAKEAWAY — Your list of references is very important because it gets beyond the barrier of the HR department to put a prospective employer in touch with someone who will give you a rave review.

BEFORE YOU GO...

Please remember to take just one more minute to write a brief review, and hopefully give my book a 5-star rating.

☆☆☆☆☆

www.ingramcontent.com/pod-product-compliance
Lightning Source LLC
Chambersburg PA
CBHW070543030426
42337CB00016B/2323